ANTHEM

THE NATIONAL POETRY SERIES

The National Poetry Series was established in 1978 to ensure the publication of five books annually through participating publishers. Publication is funded by the late James A. Michener, The Copernicus Society of America, Edward J. Piszek, the Lannan Foundation, the National Endowment for the Arts, and the Tiny Tiger Foundation.

2000 Competition Winners

Jean Donnelly (Washington D.C.), *Anthem*
SELECTED BY CHARLES BERNSTEIN
PUBLISHED BY SUN & MOON PRESS

Susan Atefat Peckham (Michigan), *That Kind of Sleep*
SELECTED BY VICTOR HERNÁNDEZ CRUZ
PUBLISHED BY COFFEE HOUSE PRESS

Spencer Short (Iowa), *Tremolo*
SELECTED BY BILLY COLLINS
PUBLISHED BY HARPER COLLINS PUBLISHERS

Rebecca Wolff (New York), *Manderley*
SELECTED BY ROBERT PINSKY
PUBLISHED BY UNIVERSITY OF ILLINOIS PRESS

Susan Wood (Texas), *Asunder*
SELECTED BY GARRETT HONGO
PUBLISHED BY VIKING PENGUIN

Jean Donnelly

Anthem

NEW AMERICAN POETRY SERIES: 37

SUN & MOON PRESS
LOS ANGELES · 2002

Sun & Moon Press
A Program of The Contemporary Arts Educational Project, Inc
a nonprofit corporation
6026 Wilshire Boulevard, Los Angeles, California 90036
www.sunmoon.com

Distributed in the United States by Consortium Book
Sales and Distribution, 1045 Westgate Drive, Suite 90
Saint Paul, Minnesota 55114-1065

10 9 8 7 6 5 4 3 2 1

FIRST EDITION
Copyright ©2002 by Jean Donnelly
Biographical material ©2002 by Sun & Moon Press
All rights reserved.

Excerpts from this work were previously published in *The Germ,
The Hat, Kenning, Lagniappe, So To Speak,* and *Volt.*
The author also would like to thank the poets and administrators of
Bridge Street Books, The District of Columbia Arts Center, Just Buffalo Literary Center,
The Poetry Project at St. Mark's Church in the Bowery,
The Ruthless Grip Poetry Series and The Mary Cotton Fund for Woman Poets
for their support.

Design: Katie Messborn
Typography: Guy Bennett
Cover art: Man Ray, *Promenade,* 1916

LIBRARY OF CONGRESS CATALOGING IN PUBLICATION DATA
Jean Donnelly [1968]
Anthem
ISBN: 1-55713-405-7
p. cm — Sun & Moon Press
(New American Poetry Series: 37)
I. Title II. Series

Printed in the United States of America on acid-free paper.

Contents

A Bonnet Gospel

Firetrucks for the second time this week at the psychiatric institute. Jack watches them like curious bobbles in a backyard. Yesterday I felt like me again. Lost all the post-pregnant physiology. Mostly in my face. The tricky and suspect Wittgensteinian theory of meaning begins in the home.

Probably when a child an infant learns object permanence. A parent is more than a cultural conveyance. But sometimes you don't feel that way. All the catalogs in the mail heave an emotional illicitness. Arthur's grouchy but tries. We don't have cash for Alex's lunch and that really upsets him. Jack climbed clad in a diaper up the stairs. A gospel is a curious maven. How do epigraphs engage the poem.

A little maitre d'. No natural world surrounds me. It butts up against the city in pockets and niches. When the latent beauty of a thing catches. That's when we can see it. But that's empowering a thing. And things can be empowered. Like the knickknacks in a catalog. Pregnancy is pure differentiation. Between beings.

And being. Remember that song from *The Sound of Music* when the child interrupts to say *But it doesn't mean anything!* A disembodied refrain of contemporary American culture. That poor door is a long flower with an ear. Who will your baby be. Freshly a person. With curious habits. With important emotional attachments. Indelible little spirit at first. When it's most vivid perhaps. Not another you.

But with little bits of you. Making a song with what no-one sees of you. Reading Mayer got me crying and laughing because you never read or approach the pregnant days with such companionship. Jack climbed from his crib today and fell on his eyebrow. Sometimes I feel sad or relieved at night that the kids are asleep. Or both sad and relieved at once.

Like feeling astounded and relieved by a poem because it changes the way you *see* the world. (See Bernstein on Oppen.) And paves the way for possibility in your own work. That's so strange how we talk in third person to the children. Not I yet. To them. Not free of them. But related.

Becoming to know that. How can you say the music shunts because it doesn't. Unless it's bubbly. All the static is important. It's intrinsic to a domestic poetics. Jack dances in a wobbly swaying way. The same way to Schubert as to *All Saints*. And Alex likes that. It's not so strange to love a song about Jesus when you're not a Christian. Mayer and Notley implode the confessional because the site of the personal meets a linguistic frontier it's bound for. Also they're brilliant. We're living over John.

Who's an accountant for the government. Big noisy family over John's head. Jack chirps when he brings me the broom and the dustpan. A little song about sweeping. When you look at your child and see a parade. A parrot. And the child again. Who he is.

Who is he. Person you thought you knew. Cleaning diapers. Carrying the first teeth in your wallet. Then you must write,

And they can't give you the time. Because it's not theirs. Or it is theirs. And the little rings they leave in the sink are innumerable. Or they cry in the night. Or call your name in the morning.

I mean your real name. Not mom. And you stop in the hallway and think about that. That they're separate. That they're separate houses with a little life going on in a parlor. Divine in a bed you said. Not a poem but a rapture. To put the title *poet* on any application. We draw the blinds for intimacy on the couch.

So that the insane inmates can't watch us. Even in daylight I wonder how far you can see in a home. Metonomy is a brilliant linguistic tryst the corporations have usurped. And we rifle through the list of presses. Because they've mixed with the poems. The critical essays on Mina Loy and Mayakovsky. An enchanted action between the fingers. How do you go about naming a child.

With lists and a sound that follows them in the playground. The employer's mouth. The two-year-old loved to twist her mother's hair while nursing. Now she tears her own out. A quirky simulation of comfort. The habits of families. Reading William James. Moving to another room in a home to see what time it is. Where's your hand. There's your hand. Jack in a sleeve makes it a hand. You can draft a poem.

And you can draft a son. Surely it will rain today. The bridge of matter upon which petit-bourgois theatre is love. Matrix of the extraneous. The paper truck driver delivers paper items to the psychiatric institute. Twice a week. We are funny in the morning chewing suspenders with growls.

Arranging the stuffed animals for effect. The gerund is a temporal conveyance. Its repetition sounds like a rock song beginning with *you*. Your brilliant poem *Politics* enacts that product of suppression. Labeling a poem political because it knows what isn't meant to be told.

A weak-kneed excuse for irrelevancy. Or Reznikoff's *Holocaust*. Which I still haven't finished. Because it's terrifying. And that's political. Not finishing it because it's terrifying. My dad says they nicknamed another pilot in Vietnam *Animal*. Because he ate the heart of a raw one. The Americans had hunted for real meat.

I thought that sounded like a movie. He said the man died in a mission he was supposed to have flown. To rescue Americans in helicopters. Alex is building a simple machine for science called *the fish-on-the-floor-feeder*. For lazy fish who'd rather not swim to the surface. The lyric circumscribes evidence. Mayer's letters tack a temporal language of fertile bother to the fore. I know Jack is hungry when he takes the jam jar out of the pantry and puts it on the footrest of his highchair.

A red glass hunger flag. Yesterday they chased one of the inmates. Down the street. On foot. In cars. A passel of professionals seeking to recover their charge. What happens to friends when they have children. It narrows. Because of constant tugging. Can't hop on out to see you. No deposits of great gulps of time together.

At least not for awhile. The glum twigs and muddy debris lie at the corner of the patio. The passive banter of choking shrubs and resilient trees. Wanting my father to see how beautiful the children are. I smile broadly. Conversations about the new mayor are tinged with a civic hope. But no-one was meant to live in a city. While your baby wonders in your womb.

Firmly rooted to that immutable sky. When you're bright and airy and not thinking of your parent's illnesses. A little rattle at the circumference of the day propels me at the next one. They said in the child's book to greet the day with gratitude.

But when it's forced Alex sees it. Yesterday Jack identified his body parts with prompting. So he knows his body's not mine. Or part of me. Little "nnn" sound when he touches his nose. There are days Arthur and I don't speak with each other. Days we're riddled by an expanse of ourselves. Or the administration of a family. Once in a while from a sulky dismissiveness.

Though mostly watching the days together. Behind ourselves. When you're pregnant you can't imagine not ever being pregnant. Days proceed on the calendar like epochs. That someone will be in the world. When you're not. Or not pregnant. Then the same sense recurs when they're infants. You can't imagine them needing less of you.

Though they do. And you're there. Now who are you. Padding parts of years with endeavor. Abutment of the household river. The quiet family in the car at the gas station. Alex wrote *I love you like the largest angel in heaven.* A dynamic of scavenging poetics. The threshold of the civic is a mother. The domestic is a political spine and cultural conveyance. *A family is tenderness.*

A family isn't always tenderness. Alex said *What kind of fate did you get. Mine's throwing confetti.* Equivalent of a baby. Equivalent of a parent's eye. All the medical pamphlets say labor and childbirth. But labor is childbirth. Like a sentence can't happen. Without the verb. The work. Oppen's verbs are rare and usually forms of *to be.*

To be in labor is a separate being human. Like being born. Or dying. There is a grammatical parallel between the infinitive and pregnancy. (See Mayer's letter lists.) When you trace your birth to your mother's body can you imagine that presence of mind. The hours spent considering you. In an abstract.

And in relation to some idea of herself. What would it have meant to her in a dress. Or winter day. How different maybe from your own maternity clothes shopping. The relevant need to surpass the state. Reach a finish. To meet you. But the horse's foal is cleaned too. And the dainty spider's eggs placate the ledge. A gestational space like the poem's. Accompanied by the days. And the visitors. Everything else is passing. While *the human abstract* is a fringe in the mind. The first time a child hands an object over. Like god. A poetics of profound irrelevancy.

Legend

(an alphabet for Alex)

little flags marking dreams come off the map
—ARKADII DRAGOMOSCHENKO

Aa

the little king says
a flag a flag a flag

the little king says
the prey of a civic map

the little king says
round me a belly
the oaths of my jury
the sum of each hoof

the rooms I leap from
to kiss you

my armor my
shadow

Bb

dear you is a fable

a tree-lined evidence

rooms for the public

rooms for a brother

a surly map of delay

& beyond the original spell

of flags of what is owned

the alphabet dreams of guests

Cc

the lions have noticed
a lens in the rushes

an equivocal badge
to science their shadow

they know a gaze allows
nonsense to unravel

generations
pilot their gestures

the collars lecture all day
in the bushes they drowse

at twilight
in the original cradle

Dd

it's a twig shield
a kind of rowdy lily
like bread splinters
found alone in coats
bellowing flirt
in a moody frame

dear you

at the center
are tables tokens
children
put together
pinched
from sun

Ee

at any rate evidence instructs
it profits unequally I said

as real as this house

lying down across the street
our trash smells sweet

Ff

the message is a shelf from it
itself it says the prey of an original
what is exempt from oaths
(*dear you*)
what more is a flag from the message
the prey of an original
itself a shelf from it

Gg

a rasping horn
collects wonder

a happy collar
science

the lonely goblin
adores it

like a sword
a greeting

a map
of his cradle

Hh

insofar as this letter finds you

tooth mad & quick I am

saving all your lectures I can't

describe the monkey each

hoof is equivocal the lens

a flat net or crisis I

adore you you know that

Ii

the little king says
hand me a mirror
he is handed a mirror

the little king says
there are guests in every room
there are guests in every room

the little king says
our rooms have shadows
our guests have shadows

the little kings speaks
softly to his shadow
the little king is

laughing
in every room

Jj

the road &
road the jury is

a badge the flag's
spell in the clamor

in the buildings some
sum of tickets

tokens the flag
snaps the children

know a sort of
sleep the public

houses the civic
homes the road

& road the shoes
their map

Kk

maybe it's a ship at twilight
maybe the swimmers on board
carry a kind of handkerchief

a lip or seam of stars might
go on behind it
the ship

maybe speech among the swimmers
is a kind of steady gaze
oblivious laughter

then the flag maybe
a kind of wintry cloth
a starry brocade

maybe the swimmers mean
to return with or without it
the ship

Ll

a brother to his
shadow they were
lions they were
to be noble
pious owning
no flag nor
oath resolute
speculative pacing
a coast where
fruit trees through
the lens shine
like armor

Mm

the message parts are
two two
parts are the message

the message our two
parts parts
our message too

Nn

the swimmers clamor
past the buildings
horns in their shoes
shoresand in their
hair a happy netting
about the party deliberate
sum of their saying is
not allowed but cast
from their souls which
glow when they share
food or fables

Oo

the little king says
why do pawns
click in my fist or

why does a sword
find its cradle

what is the original
crisis or what is

prayer
to the jury

how does my armor
grow a lecture or

the roads
their oaths

the little king says
shall I rock in the lens
for safety

Pp

your pockets I am told

are false not fold not

author a lonely goblin

format wearing a tender

ship worse than dodging

justice when the message

performs like a coast

Qq

the guests are stony
or false or tender they

pray with handkerchiefs
& shine with objective

candor *they were waiting
to be noticed* in a mirrorland

quick with their little spells
they wander through rooms

stingy with gazes their wonder
wears a training to be loved

Rr

flags here
make a stitching
sound a rugged
humming
to home

Ss

it's elective
prey as
object small
birds at
the throat
of twilight
in sight of
the little king
warning it's
you *dear*
you stingy
ideal
imitating
the horizon

Tt

the little king says

a happy tender thief in me
chases lions by the sea

(a little hollow skirt rhyme
fastened by a guest of mine)

Uu

or the kid landscape
more grave & exact

than expected unless
it grows enormous

I'll say the false errand
exists with it found

marching I'll say
maybe their king is coming

Vv

evidence is delay
is blind is
behind its singing

small birds shimmy
in a bath blotting
the plum-like dust
with candor

the days all types
viscous
with water

Ww

ice shines with laughter
in a wedge in a drift
on the shore the coast
of a mirrorland where
the goblin traps
light by the weight
of a home in the history
of its mirror its badge
of crisis wrought
in a coat of fireflies
he has said to himself
I can speak only
with someone
who holds my hand

Xx

yet says the lonely goblin
in a stony tree

in the crux of a mirrorland
notice my

technique my string
of objective fruit my

lions in that hatless
gesture each

faulty poem is a pact
in a mirrorland

won't you
says the lonely goblin

also in a mirrorland
be my book my

brother my
little king

Yy

expect a swimming price
for tricking the obvious
expect a brother's fable
to cast a soul horizon
strings of shattered poems
of sleep & ships & kid bellies

dear you

say all our tombs are cast
in a civic adventure
a flag they hover
might tousle an ocean
really only lined
with children

Zz

lion-hearted nuzzle
in a blurb mine

moral atoms
in a stony net

tongue cleansing
a lion gesture

darning it-system
hum with ink

Ballad

It rains today, my
son's singing love songs of this country
— ALICE NOTLEY

Leslie says, "something is terribly wrong, and everything else is right," five years ago before Jack and Jonas arrive through us stage to world new people into drama our particular intimacy like boxwoods keeping us in or out or bordered exclusive love affair with her ears when she tells me "the rich man from next door saying I was a beautiful woman with a beautiful name so I told him I was a man with the name Bob."

Ted said, "it's just a little dinky little poem…it says, you're either a sheep or a shepherd. And, like, you are a sheep until you get grown up, then you're either a shepherd or a dead duck," bald liability bald in the words bald when I meet him in the poems and shames me to have thought trashed in me when shepherds are out in my attic self bleating coronary path past ducks I thought they were ducks *but the light of other lives* when he said "you need company to be alive."

Jack says, "help put leaves back tree please," his second anthem autumn with warm knowing weather that the trees will shed anyway and my stress to hear it while trucks pass clean as rats smock of a smuggler he carries fruit to his father from my messy hands says "water play please clean."

Bruce says something stupid about younger poets and that's a dead divisive duck anyway ancient exclusionary mantle trophy building hee-haw party aw shucks but his poems.

My father says the war reads William James Krishnamurti runs in a pale blue hat without insurance says the war saves his grandfather's poems hates golf watches hurricanes says they respect veterans in the small town mountain out of the blue view with corn-eating deer and stray dogs loop of light and rock behind him holding hands with his second wife through Southeast Asia little bits of time hoarded past it in the mountains he keeps giving me.

Sarah said she wanted to kiss me I said no why is a school I paint to listen to something terribly wrong but not me or her when to grapple is what makes us maidens.

Susan says history and it's all the same time when you find it I can't come out of the nose-bleeding sense before or after the event where it bruises the great awning part in me that was born *a housed reputable beginner* and goes out in days corporal with different clothes in traffic with children to show how or why we listen.

Alex says, "I can't be anything right," washing pizza dishes loving his brother in a self-made voice the trouble with U.S. history pasting definitions from the curriculum remote in a way from the dawn he beats to giggle at the bus stop says chicken funny for his friends for me.

Alice says, "the problem of America is my body," and it is
and it's mine too pure arcane arc and hive breast won't be it
say you're all set create this physician with it it's not up in
the air but I'm fighting for it to alight on branches with bees.

Arthur says he dreams his family how to repair it with twine
Saturdays when we're not working but it could be this poor
door with a long flower with an ear.

Joan says "welcome to poetry" shakes my pear but my pen's
a woman bridled to gargle the insignifiprint while the hours
crawl up my back I think her mind's beautiful and thorough
and we will last of life when speaking doing with words what
I find more here.

George said "to speak of trees" what they shed or see every-
thing that's the point and to brush this tawdry suburban
into me perfect armor of insufficient wealth dormitory fable

ourselves and to things but it's primitive even to giggle with my sons when parents have or have not killed up on the hill in a house behind a country I call into them have heard or shed when we need it.

Anthem

for Rod

villainous handkerchief
of coastline

& crabtraps buckled
with miles of lilies

& lost socks
in Delaware

Leslie turns the music up
how does one country

prepare
for invasion

or strap a border
with an angry smell

pieces
of the moment

stay to gender
perception

& nourish
the air

with authorship
for the dead

a poem's nation
hitchhikes between chapels

is lonely between
structures trades

the postcards
from Arkansas

for the ottoman
for free

strains of gates
course

at the landscape
where

we lock is
poorly heard

we are where the blush is fading
recriminatory *gee* in the social battery

not understanding July in Texas
cheerleaders insist it's a sport

the remuneration of athletes
& diaper service drivers wood

crying out the point
the product

of geological love sunlit captures
the density transforming

anxiety to a civil salutation
embroidered in the curtains

how many states
can you clearly sing

Melville the criminal
in Maine by a wood

stove maybe a donut
& a hotel pen water

works the mountain
in a more

dignified language
even urban parcels

usurp the bleak
translation

paintings
in a drug store

that frame
the human

irrelevance
to land

masses good-bye
I waved

to the names
of mountain flowers

the cinematic sense
in Kansas

therefore
lawn care points to

privilege scanty
ecstatic kingdoms

magazine racks
microwave

instructions while
the funeral

traffic passes
the short wave

radio junkie
the tourist

in a Sox cap
a pretty quiet

column
of cars &

acres
of restlessness

inventing your jealousy for nature
the persons you admire

in monotony seeking love
for your intellect

Rhode Island distributes the poetic
monarchy like Robin Hood

a pasture of language to graze
or pass with indifferent

attention to the self in travel
indeed you green the crowd

with bobbing friendliness &
a cagey retention of its rooted shadow

Montana predicts
the height of chairs

& the sunflower genus
lodged in a gritty

window postcard
bottom filled creek

of usual farewells
merchants say

good-bye too their
burden of witness

is corroboration
an air of darning

houses kid engines
a metaphysical flag

it pulls & whittles
my starry pledge

outside the trees
are empty

the equivalent
of sufficiency

is being awake
that calling-mommy

voice clogging
Arizona with

an incomplete
inscrutable

water ribbon
singularly

a mansion
excess both

wrists are
myself

at risk
a sea problem

haunting the sky
a sunlight

we could anchor
disorder in also

a lozenge
of epiphanic bliss

toward the river
thinks my tongue

to translate the sense
of my child's lap

independent as a cloud
or the force of images

Mississippi church
sign *God's last name*

is not damn a limit
of signals glee

in a future corpse
heroes scar me too

refrigeration units
abduct the stillness

a sno-cone pilgrimage
to Nevada's ski-trail

happy-time barbecue
wacky permanence

of adored conviction
birds days their

heap & blessed
a raft of trivia

to harness awakeness
function of rock &

limbs tiny portraits
of events cavort

& glint doors undo
a blank emphasis

love sees Olson in New Hampshire
so *something* in the proportions

of awareness
he's a graph of ethics

for the inferred world where
chipmunks burden the lawns

& begging sense is a kinship tongue
do we correspond (not really

but in a hands-off perhaps) feigning
freedom in a formal field of power

that couple came back
from Minnesota

with a baby
alarm dinks the traction

of snowtires
& faultless satellite dishes

when have I been said
in a son's voice

to be a trilling
minute a painting

of fatigue a roar
in the poem is abstract

like *childhood* squall
of complete occurrence

broad sexual
sun in a bulb

in the peopleness
of imitation

noisy compass
& everyday

there's a toad
in the road

so I'll change
all that

about me my
tents we're

armored
by the rain

in Washington
state where

the elderly man
taps the deck

& whistles while
the macaroni boils

involve the children
in a bigger fence

of reference
like colors moving

somewhere happy
Nebraska

at 3 a.m. a motto
for money in glass

spies there itch
with honor

fatigue in the earth
a collective

spiritual project
in banners of wheat

& cows who crunch
before electric

scum
& gunshots

cannot that house
possess a place

when being human
fills the attention

of a bicycle or
Utah as eager

foot-prints back
the one-word

greeting & the lyric
bounces from dis-

ease comes to find
the tiny cloud of

common friendship
fear in a body

is an echo of past
nakedness tripping

with an alphabet
more loyal than me

the person is
a boulder without

sleep is a harbor
to be named is

action anti-sign
anti-record new

babies are people
who wake in the night

with who they are
right there

in the blue funky
nightscape or

New Mexico dappled
parallel music while

stars at sunlight
clock the blur

anti-inevitable
anti-example

you rally my expectation harbor
a slip for loss & a slip for income

versatile boats pulling leeward
through the present which is

perfection because its mother is
time's luckless candor a cartoon

precision develops the fire hydrant
distance Oklahoma inters

the memory of North America
bridge building methods movie star

bathroom minutes every tunnel
construction death pledging

the same things I sort
when I ask or pray or raft

with my pebble with
children because they barter

indeed a surface of boundaries
is irrevocably hoarse

North Carolina's pinwheel anthem
hammock factory of the mind

not a nation's swell with we in it
but a sulky magic

& a bunch of cabins
not anything a spell could worship

most children enjoy the sound of their own voice
let's go look at something & talk about it

the Indiana skyline for example its brave
400 year old tree a tin of tobacco (we weren't

meant to move our bodies faster than they can
carry our souls so they arrive a bit later

which explains the sense of delay & growing
accustomed to foreign places) children are also

kind kindly for real reasons of kindliness which
throws us a bit when we expect them to share

I heard *O Canada*
for the first time

in South Dakota
or at the World

Series which
prevents me

from easily
correcting

the national
glossary method

an American
lion is

weeping
with chastity

absent his
brothers absent

the metaphysical
poetry of his

former tribe
while an arithmetic

of honest
reason

pleasures
the prairie

miles of Whitman
bare Kentucky's

technical
population

innovative doctors
of love with band-aids

& good lord horses
but more than that *I can*

say more the domestic
event wears an alphabet

too stooping at
the boy bath with rigor

anybody breaks
the water to sing

Michael & Lizzy
are out on the porch

not their hands
in the talk

but the bluebells
& the columbine

& he watches
her talk

with a fly-
swatter

spinning
California

the truth is
thankful

'cause
he listens

how do I look beside madness
a bit lemony & all cluttered

to pledge is not a sound
to follow a flag a long pause

in the photograph Iowa's
industries in birth & death

choosing the perfect awning
to part in a mother's body

extends a civic frontier
a banner calling me to kneel

nothing magnificent
translates

dissatisfaction
seagulls on the soccer field

woman shot in back of head
rabbit hutches trash compactors

giant pecan trees
all populate

the fondly local while
commentary

demands a face
a bewildered

aesthetic figure
loose at the landscape

Missouri's quick glow
of sorrow anything

mouthed or mentioned
with gentleness

stepping gingerly through games of loitering
wealth & clothesline-yard-equipment-litter

I would almost say yes Rod
the veil of community lights New Jersey's

mystical bustle while clicking electric
meters are alone at the back of buildings

a snake in the cattails has left her young
safe with their concentrated venom

electronic hunger & the joints
of outside Colorado's parcel of scrub

& rock thought remits the scratchy
underside of patience

heavy with snow cloud exemplifies
the states pastures borders small breeding

boundaries what wants to happen means
where we meet

children in the hours too under clouds
still hidden with their eyes closed

that we have nothing bare
means we are restless

the mind is a fist in repose
a pebble slipped from a lemon

the next morning he appears
sad in blue pants in Massachusetts

he says the ancient future rags on him
not one thing makes me quicker but you

request the body
to placate itself

it giggles at you
meet the children

with a form of yourself
reserved for children

they'll giggle too
it's all one big request

interrupted by cigarettes
& airplanes & the need

the buy more _____
New York pigeons sigh

in the underground
parking garage

like a small drum
in the poem

that weeps
clicking open

a surly sound
blots on the map

for idols
what are you sending

into the sky so lovely
with your mind

not all fifty states
can be beautiful

can they also
the broken dress

the homecoming
racket when I face

Virginia I can smell
the South like the face

of Willa Cather
someone's

getting born
& the tops of trees

are nibbling
at The Poem

roots of the island
of sorrow ambulant

roots follow the car
accident giant screen

advertisements borrow
Hawaii's children real

animate monuments
burgeon the highway litter

carnation crosses with names
pass moments angular

purposeful violent flags
those peach-colored irises

from the wedding a profound
calm in the land between cars

my true stories won't cower
they're mocked

by themselves they're not
titanium-laden a furious

aerial view of North Dakota
all my errors are old with

new gadgets to entice them
their same shadows

relate love that true
luxury is convenience

they're not clockwise
they're graceful like a face

homes above the fields
the roots

durable faucets
the robes

flecks of chrome
threading

concrete watching
a clock

in Vermont hapless
din

in the bough's
sap

bless
the pottery

behold
the nursery

take
the people there

or their wonders
fine

like a minnow
wavers

mine too
children

above us
like the calendar

the sex offender's counseling group
files out of the gabled entrance

without speaking accustomed
to speechlessness

the framing guy from Illinois disregards
the honeymoon photos

the strip mall pedestrians
in the window wind

slapping the bathroom exhaust fan
Styrofoam cups on the toilet tank

wobble while perfection approaches
lurid & wishful

pendulous arcing bark of the wiener dog
battles the Bell Atlantic vortex

the habits of faces a dumpster purchase
a gift fence whatever

among the flowers in Connecticut
the boy's boarding school

aura of difference
I believe their debris

& the rainy lake day when all at once
the children think of kissing

can you be you in any state
whole sections of the nation

people won't tread funny hair
weird wrinkles with which

to love the future where are
the twins we let go Lorine

grief for the never will have been
clutches the sides of the moment

I can't help but pick flowers
I'm human I'm aloud for you

in the poem leaning
on the guardrail on the ferry

to Louisiana happy nods
to the north retreat with vowels

buckets of kudzu to douse the memory
the twin lives of words

why it's a poem not
a person not Pepsi

pills a baseball airport-
taxi-van the circumference

of longing useless
to deny it

graciousness truth
as it pursues it

them the lights
in Idaho like stars

the solace
of a map the night

living life at earth
curtains by the wood

the river the kitchen
verbal violence

derby or quiet
people the poem

where it stands
at a voice

patient
to be heard

hope apprehends
a descant pilgrim failing

the chokecherry back lane
of Alabama's mercurial

goblet of tyranny
history is intimate

with a body heaving
a map at my skin

all alive up here
sings the ground

where I step
in Wisconsin

loons break the water
like script

& worth is a raft
tossed by a witless

wrath (anyone
pledges their reasons

to it) throwing proof
to the possible ground

o.k. led the talk
like *um...*

& trumpets
slimy hinges

in the engine
poets in Florida

too though
the costume's

crowded
nevertheless

wasn't my arm
singing Dickinson

a drab decade
to share

in the Everglades
pronounced

porch-with-legs
he called

teeth *a grill*
I bitter

the slipping
forest Emily

not for clarity
though it aches

Georgia is a photograph
of my little sister

a song she plies
in the lettuce garden

a little mission
fraught with anchors

the dawn pocket faces lunch
barreled everywhere & stumbles

at the city (labor
we'll call a bride)

not Wyoming my
head looking for a home

the poem borrows
clean from breakfast

not now in my nerve
city but alive

in a spangled river
reliant champion she

(the dawn) will
study the trees

it's difficult to right the lateral distance
between sensuality & captivity

even the trees remain furtive
the mustard-colored finch

the intimacy of a dress
grocer's eggs line the Ohio border

as all night in the iced rain
Black Angus swallow dark clouds

once a beautiful fuzzy pair of socks
that belonged to a gentleman

& a mailman were lost
isn't it today

because we climbed here together
what would we do without

polyurethane Pennsylvania
the digital recession of things

our vanishing instinct for thorns
oh yeah inevitably imagined

inspected policy of locked
melodic example inner

anything I unpack to act
must be light on restlessness

a labor to name or
labor as essence

I wanted to send you
beautiful gulping poems

about postmodern grace
the handles on certain cars

& sumac bark now not
everything like sailing

to Michigan in the so cold
spray won't be anything

we've done with patience
scraping the hull

with your knee counting
what's logic or nifty even

the zenith of prayer
retains a human shadow

a thorough roof a home
such a culpable thing

I am colors in a military meadow
I am mothering strength enough

to original me I am a halo
passenger a mechanism

for civic memory I am armored
with remembered friends the length

of my arm at dusk a procession
of sleeps & blinking intimacy

with a rat's reaction to violent
impulse hair & toenails

but substantively thought
which tenders the 3 billionth

atom in Alaska where my dreams
may well be preserved

by the cold shock of days defiantly
preceding the millennial rumors

boundless bounding casual love
& naked in the glittering vista

folks kiss & never
didn't in a kitchen

or a cage or
before a battle

Tennessee's
rhododendron miles

t.v. in the minivan
freaky song of

nothing graceful
banked on the parent

problem the magic
reasons we hurt & answer

will you come back
to this please

come back the shiny
floors & cabinets

football verse on the doilies
the Browns

never had a writing
program but now they're

in Maryland right next to
Cal & I am doing

careless the underside
of Catholicism

while all the saints
become palpable

West Virginia I hear you
I can't stop hearing you

selecting fragments
of everything every

past the eloquent
senator the shape

of a boy's eyebrow
people who die

or live & rock
in the mystery

of separation
language the next

spiritual plane
in which the poem

rages because Ted &
Jack & Gertrude are

dancing in it with
friendly partners

& children of course
the children

that thing is said to be free
existing in a chorus

beauty
& its figurative thought

properties
of people & valid

imaginings
a global discomfort

theatre sorrow soon
will say *Oregon*

kisses my children
for they read & write

blossoms piping their
dwelling groove O

up into electric forests
mill-town of the heart

was soot-bare
asleeping on

the tongue of the huge
river of harm while

mothers nibble a cold
dinner at midnight

generations stamp the water
with shots & breeds of rats

flat on the important beach
rocks shimmy & curl

where I come in
is *not to be sold*

not South Carolina nor even
this raging neighborhood

dressed in winter while
a civic drum washes the toys

NEW AMERICAN POETRY SERIES (NAP)

For a complete list of our poetry publications

write us at Sun & Moon Press
6026 Wilshire Boulevard
Los Angeles, California 90036

SUN & MOON PUBLICATIONS
OF THE NATIONAL POETRY SERIES